Traditional Hymns

Complements All Piano Methods
Table of Contents

	Page No.	CD Track	GM Disk Track
Deep And Wide	2	1	1
For The Beauty Of The Earth	4	3	2
Jesus Loves Me	6	5	3
Praise God, From Whom All Blessings Flow	8	7	4
Give Me That Old Time Religion	10	9	5
Amazing Grace	13	11	6
Faith Of Our Fathers	15	13	7

Concepts introduced in *Level 1:*

Traditional Hymns Level 1 is designed for use with the first book of any piano method. Some methods may label their first book as *Book 1* (such as the *Hal Leonard Student Piano Library*), and others may label their first book a *Primer*.

Range	Symbols
	p, f, mp, mf

Rhythm	Intervals
$\frac{4}{4}$ time signature	2nds, 3rds, 4ths
$\frac{3}{4}$ time signature	

Keyboard Guides

show hand placement

L.H.   R.H.

F G A B C D E
4 3 2 1 1 2 3

ISBN 978-0-634-03677-4

HAL•LEONARD®
CORPORATION
7777 W. BLUEMOUND RD. P.O. BOX 13819 MILWAUKEE, WI 53213

Visit Hal Leonard Online at
www.halleonard.com

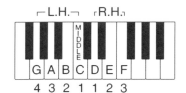

Deep And Wide

Traditional
Arranged by Phillip Keveren

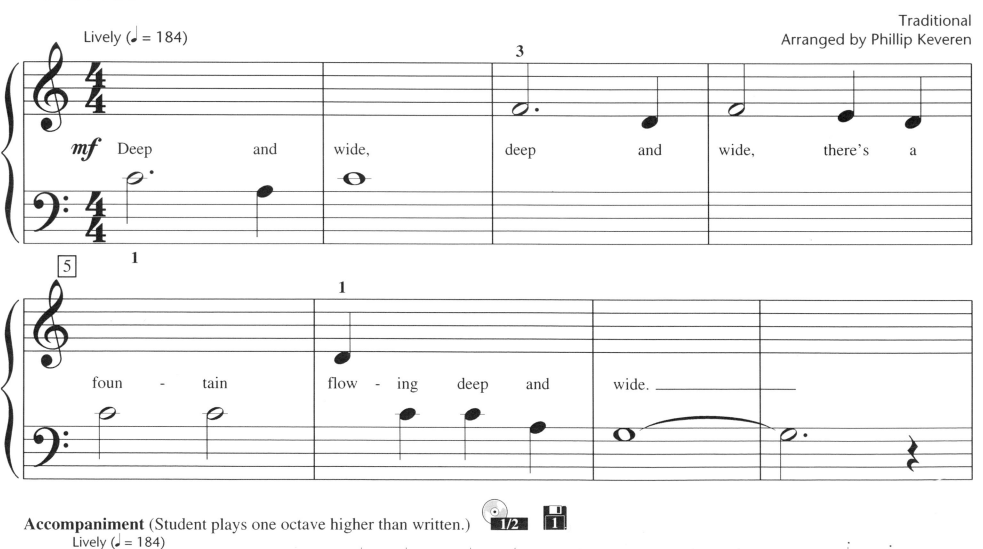

Accompaniment (Student plays one octave higher than written.)

Lively (♩ = 184)

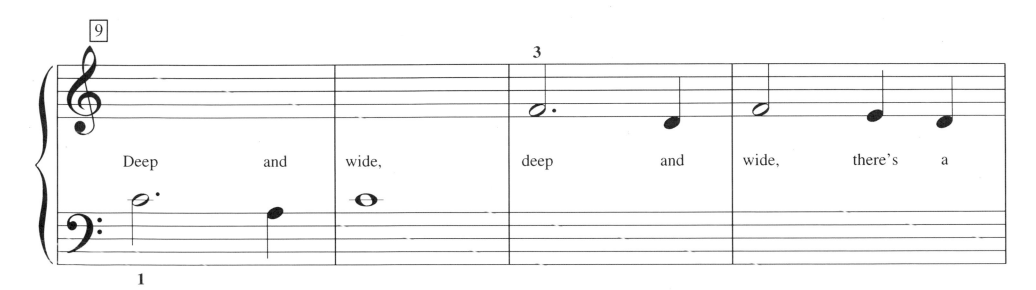

Deep   and   wide,   deep   and   wide,   there's   a

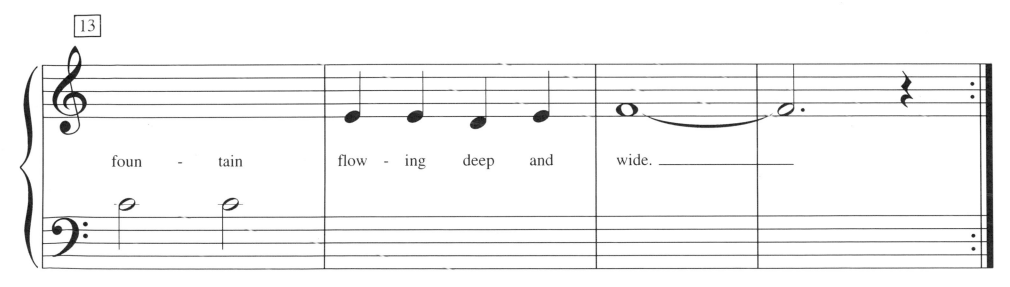

foun - tain   flow - ing deep and   wide. _____

3

For The Beauty Of The Earth

Words by Folliot S. Pierpoint
Music by Conrad Kocher
Arranged by Fred Kern

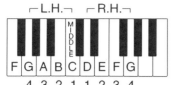

Accompaniment (Student plays one octave higher than written.)

Lord   of   all,   to   Thee   we   raise

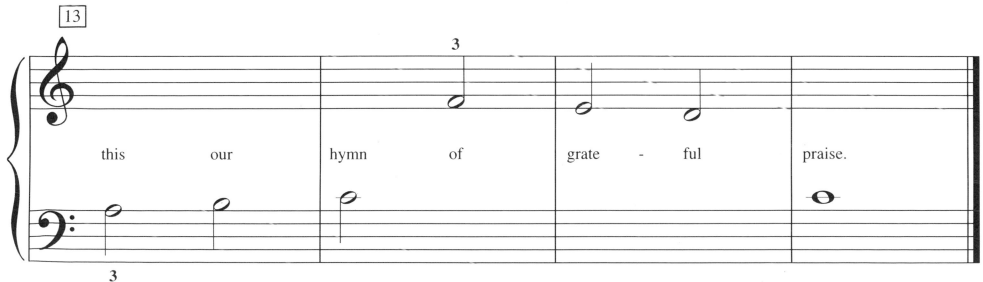

this   our   hymn   of   grate -   ful   praise.

Jesus Loves Me

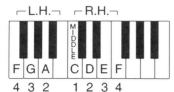

Words by Anna B. Warner
Music by William B. Bradbury
Arranged by Fred Kern

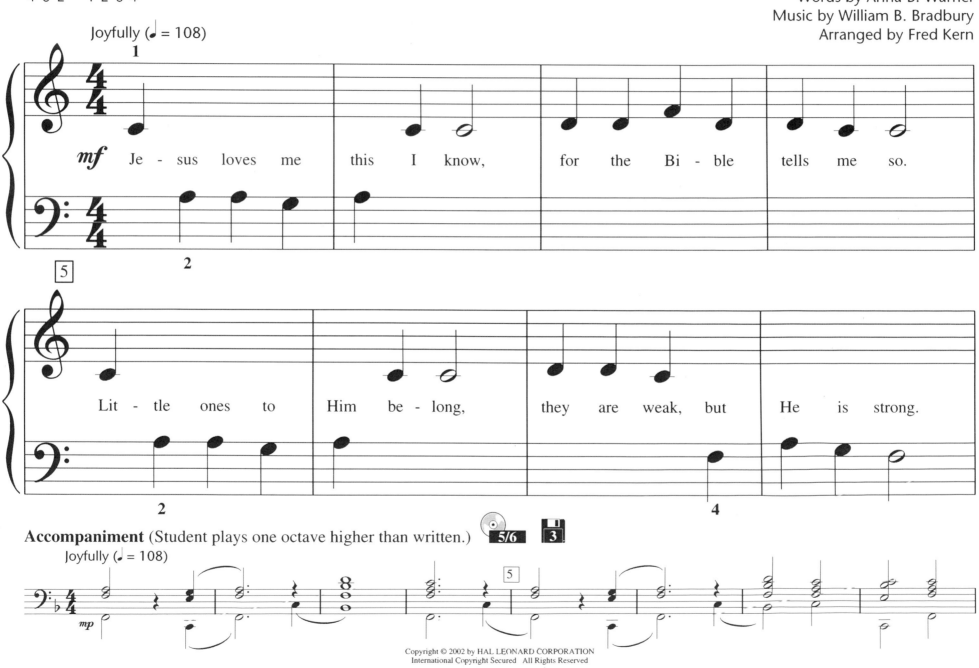

Accompaniment (Student plays one octave higher than written.)

Yes, Je - sus loves me! Yes, Je - sus loves me!

Yes, Je - sus loves me! The Bi - ble tells me so.

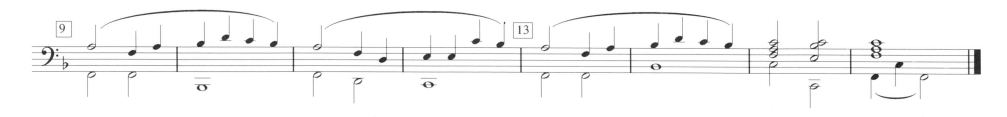

Praise God, From Whom All Blessings Flow

Words by Thomas Ken
Music Attributed to Louis Bourgeois
Arranged by Fred Kern

9

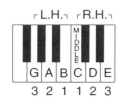

Give Me That Old Time Religion

Traditional
Arranged by Phillip Keveren

Accompaniment (Student plays one octave higher than written.) **9/10** **5**

Joyfully, in 'two' (♩ = 116)

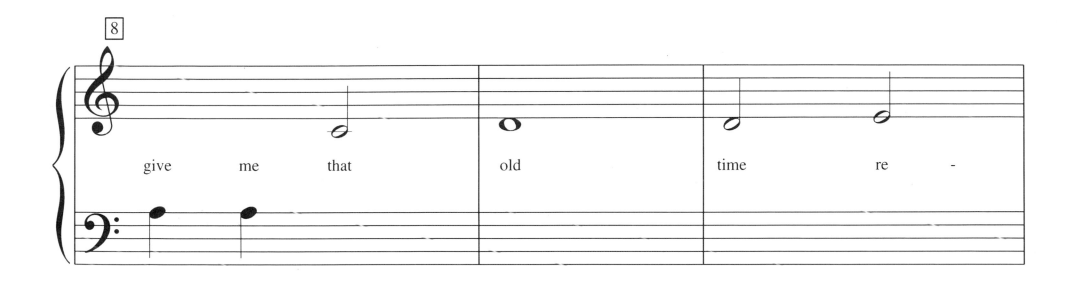

give me that old time re -

li - gion, give me that old time re -

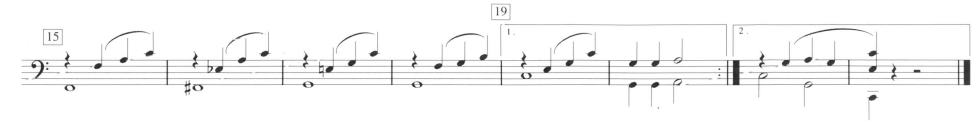

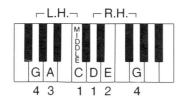

Amazing Grace

Words by John Newton From A Collection of Sacred Ballads
Traditional American Melody From Carrell and Clayton's Virginia Harmony
Arranged by Edwin O. Excell
Adapted by Mona Rejino

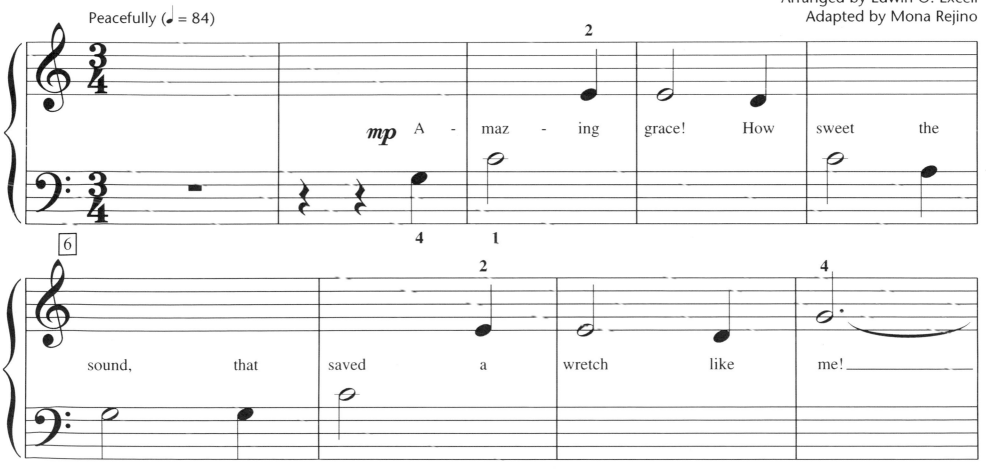

Accompaniment (Student plays one octave higher than written.)

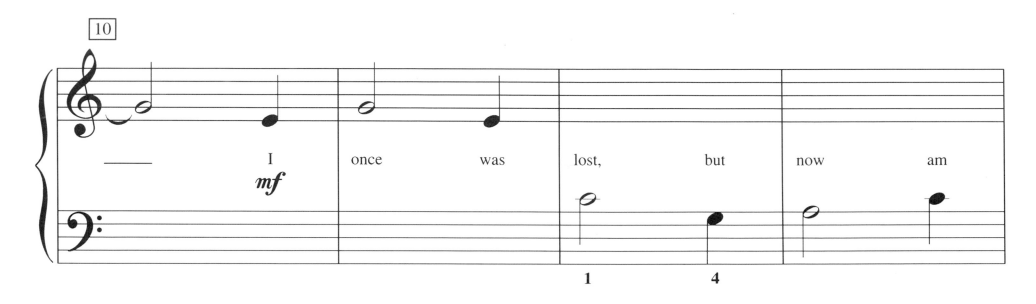

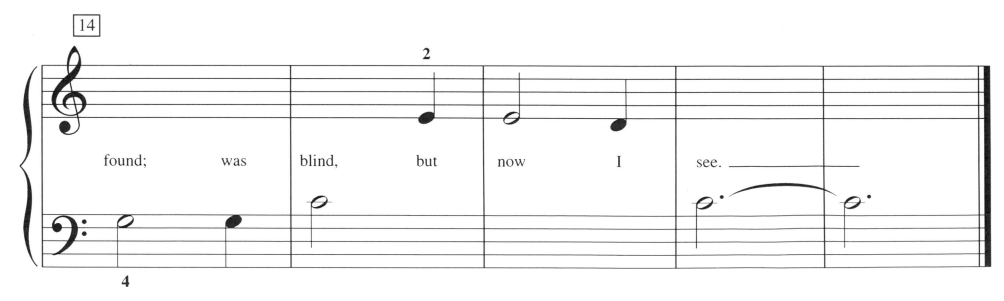

Faith Of Our Fathers

Words by Frederick William Faber
Music by Henri F. Hemy and James G. Walton
Arranged by Mona Rejino

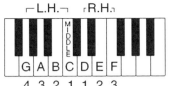

Accompaniment (Student plays one octave higher than written.)

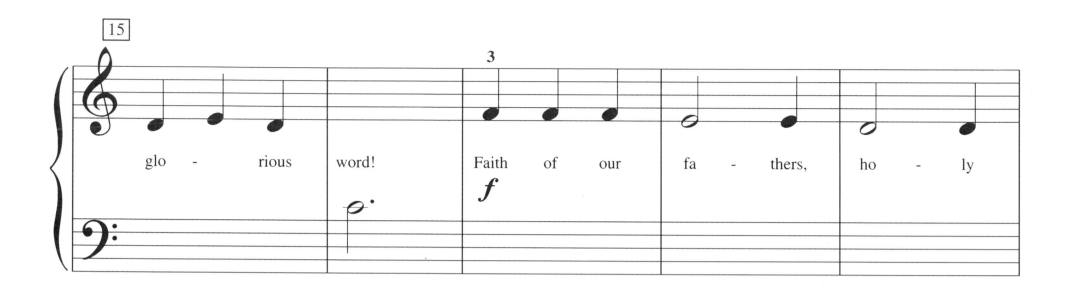

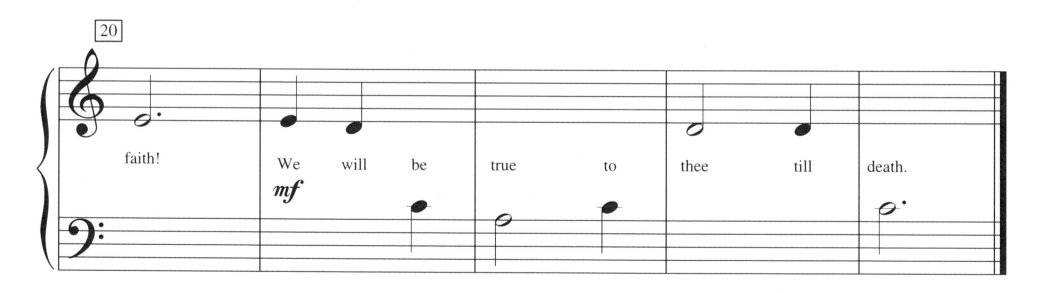